NOT SEALIONS BUT LIONS BY THE SEA

Alec Finlay is a poet and artist whose work crosses over a range of media and forms. In 2020 he was awarded a Cholmondeley award. In 2022 he completed *I remember: Scotland's Covid Memorial*. Recent publications include *descriptions* (2022), *a far-off land* (2018), and *gathering* (2018). A selected short poems, *play my game*, was published in 2023.

Also by Alec Finlay

Atoms of Delight (ed.) (pocketbooks, 2000)

Labanotation: the Archie Gemmill goal (pocketbooks, 2002)

Ludwig Wittgenstein: There Where You Are Not (with Guy Moreton) (Black Dog, 2005)

One Hundred Year Star-Diary (morning star, 2008)

Mesostic Remedy (with Laurie Clark) (Ingleby Gallery, 2009)

Ian Hamilton Finlay: Selections, (ed.) (University of California, 2012)

Be My Reader (Shearsman, 2012)

The Road North (with Ken Cockburn) (Shearsman, 2014)

Taigh: a wilding garden (morning star, 2014)

Global Oracle (morning star, 2014)

a-ga: on mountains (morning star, 2014)

ebban an' flowan (with Laura Watts & Alistair Peebles) (morning star, 2015)

I Hear Her Cry (with Stuart Clements & Jeremy Millar) (Ingleby Gallery, 2015)

A Variety of Cultures (Jupiter Artland, 2016)

A Far-off Land (with Hannah Devereux) (morning star, 2017)

minnmouth and tidesongs (morning star, 2017)

gathering (with Hannah Devereux, Mhairi Law, & Gill Russell) (Hauser & Wirth, 2018)

light is a right (with Hayden Lorimer & Hester Parr) (morning star, 2023)

I remember Scotland's Covid Memorial (with George Logan) (Stewed Rhubarb, 2024)

CONTENTS

HOMAGE TO VELIMIR KHLEBNIKOV	9
AFTER DANTE, THE INFERNO, CANTO 13	10
LET ME REMIND YOU (THE DREAM POEM)	11
(WHEN I WAS THREE, STOOD BETWEEN MUM AND DAD, BY THE TOP POND)	15
TWO CHILDHOODS	16

  KIPPERS

  YOU'RE SO BRAVE

THE NIGHT-WATCH	17
THE STONYPATHIANS	19

  SEA ECK

  LOCHAN ECK

  NEW MODEL GLIDER

  SAILING THE LITTLE BOATS

  FROM QUESTION YOUR TEASPOONS

    NOTHING RIPENED

    SUNKEN GARDEN

    BOURNVILLE

    STONYPATH SPECIES SURVEY

    [SHE REGRETS}

    RAILWAY MODELLER

    [IT TOOK THE FARMER]

    [HE SAYS YOU HAVE YOUR]

    1/300

    GUDERIAN

    EXEMPLUM

    GAME

    FISHING

    GUDDLE

A CHILD'S DRAWINGS FOR VERSES	29
FAMILY	30
INHERITANCE	31
THE MISSING ORKNEY LYRICS	32
BROKEN DISHES	33
THE LATE SHOW	35

DIE EINE	36
PRINCESS ELIZABETH WOOD	38
ANOTHER DAY	39
THE DYKER'S FRIEND	41
SWEENEY'S CALLING	43
YES, SOME INJUSTICE IS WHAT HATE LOOKS LIKE	48
PURPLE BLOOMS	49

    AN ARGUMENT

    WITH TRAUMA

    FOR FORGIVING

    IS / IN

    SHE'S A HUNTER

    A CHARM AGAINST DOMESTIC VIOLENCE

    L'ANIMA FEROCE

A DRY SPELL IS KILLING ME	61
APOLOGIA	62
DAYBOOK	63
THE LANGUAGE	67
HOW WOULD YOU LIKE (AFTER ALFRED & GUINEVERE)	68
T-H-E-D-O-G	70
BUT THAT HAS NOTHING TO DO WITH POETRY	72
AFTER FITTERMAN'S 'NOTES ON CONCEPTUALISM'	74
AFTER DOTTY LASKY	75
THE LETTER	76
LET'S AGREE	77
FROM THE SAYINGS OF CHAIRMAN MCGINN	83
TWO PLACE-NAME LOVE-POEMS	84

    THE YELLOW MOUNTAIN

    FOOL'S MIND

PLACE-NAME POEMS	87

    MAIGHDEAN MHONAIDH

    COIRE SÙILEAGACH

    ALLT PHOUPLE

    AVAGERILL

    BAD NAN DEARCAG

    ABERGELDIE

    GEALLAIG

CAMPING	90
THE CARAVAN BRIDE	91
LOCH DUILLEAG-BHÀITE	93
HUTOPIANISM	94
CARBETH	
INSHRIACH	
FOR GUY	
MEASURE FROM A MAN'S BODY	
AM BOTHAN AS FHAIDE AIR FALBH— THE FAR HUT	96
BILLIA CROO (GRID-CONNECTED WAVE TEST SITE, ORKNEY)	97
A TREE SPEAKS	100
TREES ARE Y'S	101
BE THE BEAR	102
TAIGH NA CAILLICHE	103
TWO PATHS (INSHRIACH)	104
AFTER GEDDES	106
LIONS	107
HERE'S AN EMPTINESS WE COULD SHARE	108
AVOCADO (I)	109
AVOCADO (II)	110
NOCTURNE	111
RIFFING ON ENSLIN	112
MAKE MEND	113
SADFACE	114
TWO BAYS	115
KINGHORN	
RACKWICK	
THE BIRCH	119
THE CATCH	121
POOR.OLD.	122
LYRIC	123
GRAVE POEMS	124
14.III.2011	
14.III.20	
14.III.21	
14.III.24	
ACKNOWLEDGEMENTS	129

© 2025, Alec Finlay. All rights reserved; no part of this book may be reproduced by any means without the publisher's permission.

ISBN: 978-1-917617-04-8

The author has asserted their right to be identified as the author of this Work in accordance with the Copyright, Designs and Patents Act 1988

Cover designed by Aaron Kent

Cover art by Alec Finlay

Edited and Typeset by Aaron Kent

Broken Sleep Books Ltd
PO BOX 102
Llandysul
SA44 9BG

Not Sealions but Lions by the Sea

Alec Finlay

Broken Sleep Books

HOMAGE TO VELIMIR KHLEBNIKOV

```
        S  S
    P   O  E  M
        U  N
        N  S
        D  E
```

AFTER DANTE, THE INFERNO, CANTO 13
i.m. Michael Stanley
for Carrie Stanley
'Non fronda verde, ma di color fosco;
non rami schietti, ma nodosi e 'nvolti;'

the dead fall

  into us

    – don't be afraid

to give pity

  to those

    who can't

speak   when

  grief breaks up

    the path

head back

  to The Tree

    whose scars

heal naturally

  as years

    and years

of over-

  growth fuses

    the callus

LET ME REMIND YOU (THE DREAM POEM)
'... let me remind you that everyone with a window already jumped'
— Joshua Beckman, *New Haven*

we've to bear what keeps us in mind:
the kindness of a friend who drove

all night to be near, a daughter
practised in arriving comes in time

to lift mum safe from the last bath,
the pad on the hessian bedside table

with biro lists of gifts, garden tasks
(scored out), and a plan to end pain

made, made again, but never taken.
The night she left the shock was mes-

meric. I held the bed so's not to go
out the window. I had to learn dreams:

echelons of silver planes in fingertip
rose through her air, behind where

she was waving on the – *uh-oh* – crown
of the tallest pine she must fall from.

Not to worry, it's my dream:
replay the action – fast-as-dreams-allow –

by the fifth go I've prepared a catch-
all nest for her to plummet into.

In her dream the hill she'd chosen
had a hazel whose suckers grew

in knuckle-duster loops and folds,
with an arch we took turns to wriggle

ourselves free of the muck the bottle-
smashers make. A *we do* vow

to parley her terror, to be in nature,
as she used to in our future.

Another dream had her forcing
a pitiless swim 8 miles into the bay.

I dreamed lifeguards to fetch her back.
They buried her in a pit of sand

but made sure they dug her out un-
harmed (it's my dream), and floated

her in the water, strong arms by her
sides, draped in blades of kelp

and hung with cists of air to breathe.
The pit is slim (as happiness is)

and – in a dream – becomes the cold
paragraph of sea we really dived in

when we dreamt our sea loft in Fife.
That, over there, is the same bit of sea

in my kitchen window, colouring
each lock-down day, adding a gull

on the chimney pot to repeat
how you'd laugh when we'd chant

one-leg, one-leg, cheering, for any
gull is the one if it can stand on

one-leg. If this sun-cure flops,
falling out a window or wading

in the waves – like my blind dog
paddling towards the last dim bulb

of sunset – remain options,
when there's this pain this often.

I dreamed the dog roped to a car
that's – *oh no* – accelerating. So

I dreamed a me to leap, cut, leap,
cut it free. Comforting the injury

my dream dog comforted me (muttering):
don't be so stupid, those drownings

aren't waves, but a swim to tide in.
It means something like ... you

can seep your head in water while
I bathe in an oxygen life's intent on.

(WHEN I WAS THREE, STOOD BETWEEN MUM AND DAD, BY THE TOP POND)

I drop me off the bank
directly into the deep

turn my jersey-arms
  around   in the prisms

  parting
    the turbid pond

light is
bubbling

where I keep   being breath-
ing   with-

  out
  the care   of air

lifting my head
dreading the murky limbs

which are going to reach
me out the swim

TWO CHILDHOODS

kippers
they called me

despite the smoke
from the stove

and the clothes
asleep on the pulley

I took the taint
personally

you're so brave
he said
no I'm not she said

you are he said
*you think you just
did what you had to*

as a child and that
he said *is*
why you were so brave

THE NIGHT-WATCH

that last night
you rose up
out of the curl

of morphine
asking for *nurse*
one's coming

nurse shhh I've
pressed the bell
you went red

furious said *no*!
again *nurses*! lifting
pin-thin pyjama

legs that couldn't
hold you clear
of the bed I need

to lean and shield
your rage now
go–away–you!

press the bell again
feebly smothering
you with the baffle

of a dimpled blanket
when the nurse has
settled you down

for that last sleep
I grasp that your
dying mind didn't

need a nurse's help
that it was the old
urge to go through

and charm the women
in the staffroom
one last time

no rapprochement
for us then
only the task

of keeping guard
over a possibility
that died long ago

THE STONYPATHIANS

from 'Dunsyre'

Red are the roads about the hills of Dunsyre,
And the soft spring rain is falling,
And circling slowly about the grass-green hills
The lonely whaups are calling.
  — Helen B. Cruikshank

An Autumn thought: Stonypath
  — Ian Hamilton Finlay, *Domestic Pensées*

SEA ECK

her little mast and sails
are broken and forlorn

pond mud smears and splashes
the hull that gleamed and shone

duckweeds stoop the gunnels
rudderless her windblown helm

wheels in the merest breezes,
but, glory faded, she floats on

LOCHAN ECK

I miss the skimming
  swallows
over the dark lochan

the waters where I swam
  eye-to-eye
with the blue dragonfly

NEW MODEL GLIDER

with a black bruise nose
of plasticine Dad launches

her up as she dips in cupped arcs
hiccupping over thistles

and molehills we watch her fly
and wish for a wee thermal

to scoop her magically further –
to the road or

an even more wonderful dis-
astrous landing in the peaty burn

as the tight elastic band whirrs
unwound I run after

chasing the tail in my wellies
arms out to catch at ...

... the ... moment ... before
she touches down

my ankles tumble over
–smash goes the balsa

SAILING THE LITTLE BOATS

Ailie and I are let
pick one sailboat each
to hold carefully

by its weighty keel
of lead, so's not
to break the rigging

at the lochan's shore
we slip them in lightly
and, if the wind is right,

watch together
as my zulu and her fifie
bob and tack

their angles across.
My job always
to race round the path

path, fetch them both
back when their sprits
catch in the rushes.

Sailing the little boats
never lasted long
and nothing

really happened
but for our sharing
their floating.

FROM QUESTION YOUR TEASPOONS

nothing ripened

   tiny hard pears   & wooden apples
   neat-striped green   & purple gooseberries
   like blood blisters   wrinkled golden quince

unless it was determined

sunken garden

what was grass
has filled with stones
and floats softly
mostly on moss

bournville

nail-holes in
a cocoa tin
make a fine filter
for a spring

Stonypath Species Survey

she was the *bio-*
he was the *blitz*

she regrets those afternoons
of hard scrubbing—
the words that lost
their outline of meaning

railway modeller

a family scheme
to ease our debts
collecting lichen

from the dyke
to sell in bags
as miniature trees

for the train sets
and battlefields
of model enthusiasts

it took the farmer an after-
noon to plough out

the Stone Age houses
but we kept the sheen

greenstone axe-head safe
in a drawer, with other

relics – rubber bands,
broken glasses, pencil stubs

he says *you have your*
own water here?
yes she says

he says *I kent that*
but I was told
to come and ask

1/300

that was the Christmas
of dappled snow
and a tinfoil river

made with liebe
and papier-mâché
to the wrong scale

guderian

my tortoise over-wintered
under the table tennis table,
then made a slow march

on the strawberry patch
to see out summer
as his garden panzer

exemplum

a story my father loved
was how the printer said
after a botched job

well if you wanted
it done properly
you should have said

game

plait me a tail of rushes
I'll be your tyger in the grass

fishing

set the Irn Bru
son   to cool

there   at the edge
of the lochan

guddle

would you dare
reach some fingers
right in there

right under
the grassy bank
and tickle the dark?

A CHILD'S DRAWINGS FOR VERSES

an elefant concealed among straws
  of tame camouflage

tigers and heinkels – with their punctuation
  of decals, propellers, tracer, and radios

a big rocket is firing for you, two
  little rockets are gliding for us

the plane's tail, above, in a fankle of flames
  the parachutes, below, stitched with kisses

a family of I, you, me, we,
  and *he*

a boy soldier caught up in
  the effort of war

FAMILY

father
        is the war of all things

mother's
        word is ward

family
        is a shipwreck

children
        are the revolution

INHERITANCE

this is just to say
that I have taken

the little boats
that you made

with keels of lead
and hanky sails

the fine woollen socks
your muses gave you

a dusty mouth organ
and some books

Creeley, Le Corbusier,
and *Zen Gardens of Japan*

the rest of what's left
the world can keep

THE MISSING ORKNEY LYRICS

I
Orcadian
Arcadian

red
lobster

Arcadian
Orcadian

yellow
lobster

II
a green

jersey *she*

loves me

a brown

jersey *she*

loves me

not

BROKEN DISHES

That was the week that Dad got his diagnosis
and the flowers broke that are now in shards,

the week we heard the cancer was terminal
and the flowers broke that are now in shards.

That was the week the dog went fighting
and the flowers broke that are now in shards,

the week his cheek swelled up like a fur balloon
and the flowers broke that are now in shards.

That was the week that I got the chills
and the flowers broke that are now in shards,

the week the virus became a winter fever
and the flowers broke that are now in shards.

That was the week the bloody dog bit me
and the flowers broke that are now in shards,

the week we each had our bottles of antibiotics
and the flowers broke that are now in shards.

That was the week the lid of the teapot fell
and the flowers broke that are now in shards,

the week the pieces scattered over the floor
and the flowers broke that are now in shards.

That was the week I decided to stay in bed
and the flowers broke that are now in shards,

the week there was nothing but Bach on the radio
and the flowers broke that are now in shards.

That was the week I lay with the dog
and the flowers broke that are now in shards,

the week he curled up beside me like a pastry
and our flowers all broken now in shards.

THE LATE SHOW
after Tom Paulin

The ones I felt sorry for
were the paras
those young men

in uniform
who'd been brutalised.
They were thugs

Germaine sent
in by public school-
boys to kill

innocent people
they were rotten
racist bastards!

DIE EINE
i.m Hamish Henderson

you were a great man
  vast even   to scrub
    kneeling in the bath

like a white elephant
  I push and pull *ooh*
    that's goods

with the whiskers
  of the brush
    Eck you say

this one time
  I want to risk a lie
    down

breaking dull routine
  but how will I
    lift your bulk

back up with those
  two busted hips?
    here's a Hamish lux-

uriant in load-
  bearing water
    and an Eck sat

on the loo seat
   asking about the guns
      of Alamein

and your retreat
   to Karnak   searching
   for *Die Eine*

of the poem
   in tears you quote
      Rilke's 'Tenth'

in German
   by my having none
      I gathered this

was the true purpose
   of memory
      and in the face

of fate we fastened
   hands and helped
      you back to dry land

PRINCESS ELIZABETH WOOD

at sixteen I spent a summer spell
finding the wood for the trees

as Grandad hirpled the hill
pointing his stick at each spruce

to fell that coming fall
we hacked the axe blaze

peeling a lick of bark
off either side the trunk

marking his choices:
which gets light / which falls

if I wandered the stand today
up and down the needly runs

I'd still find a few tall trees
which bear our pale scars

ANOTHER DAY
partly after Heaney's Sweeney

it's a day for
  finding other kinds
    of happiness

making honey
  of our failures
    for   at its best

the world's a nest
  at its worst
    sharp with thorn

singing
  the kettle's on
  the summersgone

brewing the heather
  tea
    in a camp kettle

an outdoor infusion
  mildly scented
    slightly bitter

passed between us
  a tonic for depression
    won't you at least

sip a few grains?
  it will do you good
    for your sadness

THE DYKER'S FRIEND
   'mindin mair strang nor stane'
    — Kristie De Garis

when the drystone
wall is 'complete'
then we begin

   the unending work
    of repair

*

the stone finds
   –who I felt I had to be

it's place in the wall
   –who I truly am

*

comes a time
   –the wound

to turn around
   – the stone

*

the sheep dyke's
lack of hearting

is a form of endurance
which keeps it standing

by letting the wind
blow in and blow through

*

after Novalis

stranger
star

you
glitter

in our
familiar

  :

  stone

SWEENEY'S CALLING
　'Bellum pacis fecisti'

I dreamt a hut
with a high thorn-bed
　which Bobby built
　among the bluebells
　　on the dark side
　of the island
where a new sun pops
　behind the peaks
　　every evening.

I dreamt the hut safe –
　with books, candles, feather-
　lined walls, and a warm
　pot stove – for Sweeney
　　to heal in.

> But such wild beauty
> 　such grooved boards,
> 　　and such kind views,
> 　　　　tilted my lover's mind
> 　　　　　to madness.

> When the *cuckoo*
> 　called from its grey rock
> 　she stole its song
> 　　bid it gone *cuckoo*
> 　　and threw out
> 　　　a *cuckoo* warning –

cuckoo resiling off
the crags *cuckoo* scaring
　away the gowk
　　cuckoo who'd never
　　　feel safe with her glam
　　cuckoo guise or wordless
　cuckoo songs again.

　　　This ringer for Sweeney
　　　　was a terrifying wraith
　　　　　of anomie smirching
　　　　　　the hut in *cuckoo* shame
　　　　　and self-loathing
　　　　warring with this
　　　place of peace.

A year on she returned to *cuckoo*
　Sweeney without me
　　　　　　translating the hut of healing
　　　　　　into *Cuckoo Island*

　　　　　　a theatre to mum
　　　　　　& mim the spectrum
　　　　　　of a father's anger

　　　　　　　　seeing into her own
　　　　　　　　sad gaze in the mirror
　　　　　　　　　of the lochan she
　　　　　　　　　　transitioned into this

             his   a him within   gazing
               back at theirself.

                A garb
             of tangled beard,
               scrob, foxing, some
               hoary lichen.

              A hairgrip with
              dark jaws screwed
              tight as a mantrap.

              Each thorn wound
              with a crazy yarn
              of goss & silk.

A-calling *cuckoo*   hear her
 cuckoo   singing   hear
  her plaintive *cuckoo*
 song   hear the *cuckoo*
   singing him *cuckoo*
  as-a-man- *cuckoo-*
as-a-woman- *cuckoo*
  as-a-bird *cuckoo* as-
such-a-and-such-a- *cuckoo*
calling *cuckoo* such a
 plume, such *cuckoo* camo
concealing a frenzy–
   tenderness, rage, tears,
     cuffs, anguish.

Like the kid I am
　I swam out
to the swan's island,
　found it floating,
unsurely, like
　a clumsy foot, hovering
　over a long-delayed
decision.

The turf of matted reeds
　was fine enough
　for buoying a nest,
　　but sharp, slithery
　　　and liable to sink a man.

　　　And, like all such
　　　　apparatus of mythic
　　　　meta-morphing
　　　　　　up close it was
　　　　　　just a mess
　　　　　　　of shit & slime.

*For some, healing
is an alluring echo.*

*For some, healing is
a reflection within
which the truth's*

locked and hidden.

*For some healing is
an accusation.*

*For some, healing
is leaving.*

YES, SOME INJUSTICE IS WHAT HATE LOOKS LIKE

the divine grace
  of the chimney piece

the weeping ash
  with its own reasons

the rainbow armband
  retuned to greyscale

all my fave records meta-
  morphosed to *vinyl*

the third child that's sure
  to buck the market

writing at *them* versus
  writing for *us*

the minister saying to his congregation
  youse are all beloved

the City of Rome giving birth
  to the wolf

an orchard where the village
  once stood

AN ARGUMENT
   riffing on Jack Gilbert

CRAZY

SHADE

 fist

PURPLE

BLOOM

 bruise

WITH TRAUMA

we're more
  the things we do

than what's been
  done to us

FOR FORGIVING

the first time my love hit me
was excused by their past

the second time my love hit me
their past became ours

the third time my love hit me
they said they were mad

the fourth time my love hit me
was just a kick on a plane

the fifth time my love hit me
was on the night I left

the last made an ending
that would have allowed
  for forgiving

IS / IN

violence is less shocking
when you live in
a state of fear

more terrifying
when you are in love
with your assailant

SHE'S A HUNTER

As we step out
from under the wood
your hand feels

for mine, forcing
a rush of blood
up my arms.

The furious hunter
who hides in
clear sight, might

they see us? Maybe
she spied your
fire tattoos,

saw our bare
kiss beneath
the shy branches?

Am I in for it again?
Just the touch
of a hand shaken

loose (finger by
finger by finger)
has shaped

the ghost fist
of twelve blows
that smithered

my heart. But
there is another
wood. And in it

there is a ring
of roots we knelt
and crept

our arses through
to prove love
could have been safe.

A CHARM AGAINST DOMESTIC VIOLENCE

                              I said
        I can't speak of
        the violence that
        went unseen
you're safe
        as none of us needs
        go unseen   let me
        say what can't be
                            am I?
        for those who know
        how it feels
        to hear the latch
(click)   *(click)*
        and feel glad
        and feel alone
        and feel afraid
                      am I safe?
        when I was touched
        a reflex flickered
        will I be attacked?
what am I?
        I didn't say no
        didn't leave
        didn't fight back
what am I?
        I didn't speak
        when soft fingers

        crushed a fist

                what are they?

        when the violent
        are blind to their
        own violence

                they are

        feeling each rage
        as another incident
        in their suffering

I'm saying

        the hurt in a fist
        is less than not
        being believed

                are you're safe?

        if what had happened
        hadn't? if what hadn't
        happened had?

I said

        what really happened?
        when I can describe
        each time

                she said

        she couldn't remember
        when she hit me   but
        she remembers one time

                what are you saying?

        that I can't remember
        she says she's sure
        there was a reason

she says

    she wasn't like this
    before what she
    endured as a child

        I said

    fists   and their acts
    are gestures
    for you to own

I'm saying

    what I can forgive
    is given in what
    I'm saying

        we're safe

    I know in time
    we will heal
    given time

saying

    we'll be safe
    we will?
    we will heal

        will we?

    we will
    when we dwell
    in empathy

I'm saying

    we will

when we dwell

in the imagination

                saying

we're safe

when the saying

has a home

L'ANIMA FEROCE
an overhearing in the underpass, Milton Keynes

who wants a truce
who owes me the time I can never get back
who wants their dog back now
who wants every dog in the world back
now who wants a truce
the choice was taken away from me
just to be able to believe in what I fucking believe in
and who believes in me
no-one
one-two-three or fuck all
no-one can hide
no subway
where's my fucking dog
no-one better breathe
or move a muscle
or they're fucking dead
no-one ever again
if I don't get what I want
my way or the fucking highway
who wants anything natural
man-made or in my fucking head
who controls nature
who controls demolition
who controls that fucking blue thing over there
who controls any machines
made by man nature anything
who tried to shut down Luton
who tried to shut down Milton Keynes

anyone working on the site at Fletchers Mews
who tried to shut down the world
now who wants a truce
who wants protection
you choose
is there anywhere safe in Milton Keynes
if you want safety
or the security of your children
who told me where my place would be
because I can't remember
who wants to live again
who can tell me where the fuck's my dog
you better stop making me make decisions
I can't make
you better get under here right now
pull those gates away
and turn this round
you've all seen the film
you said no sides
you forced me to do something
and you've got to choose
the truth now any colour
black-and-white-unite two-tone
who doesn't want to believe
any film I want to create
who wants to put this in a book
who wants to talk about suicide
where's my freedom
I want the truth here right fucking now
if you take things from me I had no choice

who thinks they're safe now
who thinks their kids and family are safe now
who is your security
who wants to play now
now who wants the truth
if you want stars to shine at night
where the fuck's my dog lily

A DRY SPELL IS KILLING ME

I still have
feelings for you
I am so idyllic

so romantic
I want love
I need a hard-

working discreet
modest humble
guy from nearby

into all styles
of pleasure
a subtle man

a man
without feeling
hinged on fun

APOLOGIA

their health being the thing
an ill person can least control

may leave them seeming
controlling : tuck the blanket

in   let them rest alone
give them their morning

tender a blessing   see their
health returning   in return

DAYBOOK

You, you don't care a kite string.

What's past is prologue. Even if the length of last night was bit with breath-knots, at last the figure of the fig is riffing behind the orange blind, and there's a fresh wash of cars daubed over the dawn radio.

The bed, it bends. The tea's on, twitter's up, and I'm in sleep debt again. All a-womble. Quanked. There's some pain. And there's the sun coming again.

The seedlings are waking to another morning of etiolation, while the slow cooker sleeps over its latest vague stew, and the plant pots still, sigh, sit in their parcel.

The drum roll from 'She's lost control' thrums through the wall. I've fallen again onto the fuck-you couch, dragging it round the room as I stalk some sun, in the buff again for no-person.

Welcome to allergy corner, where all the symptoms make weather, and all the trees propose diagnoses. Is it really a choice between victims and vitamins? Bad and good dirt?

Life got in the way of a letter that came late, and open, explaining how life is – *the chaos, the need for constant & careful curation.*

Please pass me another small pastel pill before bed, and a handful of capsules for morning.

Please twist the two rowans and plant some more stone fruits.

Please make sure they mend the gutter where the wasps get in.

Please ask them to break apart the concrete and put in an apron of pebbles, so the rain soaks-a-way safely.

Please remember to trim seven rungs off the trailing hysteria on the wall.

The Sponge is of one mind, softish, in a fold of The Bath.

Ach, there's *coughs* dampness in this house, *coughs* cockling the pages, as sure as sure as I'm a symptom whisperer, and *coughs* my illness is an IT that listens *coughs*.

Wurries yes *coughs* spores and spores of wurries *coughs* yes, they hide in the hyphae – I saw them, *coughs* I saw where they grow when we wheeled out the Ercol.

There's warning of a leek shortage. Here's more parcels sat at the door waiting to be collected. Should we mend those slates, or wait for next door's ash to come in through the roof?

Do you need pics or what? (Doesn't mean it never happened).

Yes, I bobble along. Yes, I'm further away from then.

Yes, I suppose, yes. But, somehow, I seem no nearer now.

Yes, life should be more than snuffles and scuffles.

Yes, this is the hat I live in, for now – but it's *not* a hate, and for *that* I'm internally grateful.

That, and the bit of life before *them*, when we still wore our shyness, innocent-like, in plants and games, and our wurries were what we hung out to dry, like a pair of dream beach-gowns.

The sheets on the line flap me in and out of the sun.

The chair makes a table for glasses, the stack of unread books, spare ink cartridges, bookmarks, coconut, rescue remedy, nytol, olbas, candle.

The Horizon is robust. The truth must come a long way to meet us.

So, come on old man, let's listen to another of her famous interviews with waterfalls. There, that's it: can you hear it, that's the difference between frequency and abundance.

There's feathery food, nap intimacy, buckwheat pancakes, bone stock, the sunflower on the landing, avocados walking down the stairs.

There's kindness and laughter über alles!

There's a shared thermos.

There's another church with a minister who says
mon the love.

There's a different bench for each episode of our conversation –
a blue one for hearing, a green one for listening.

There's a day as was, if you'd stuck, we could've parked
our sticks by the door and limped towards a safer life.

There's this diagnosis of chronic illness: it's when
you've been left by most of your friends.

But John would say, all an angel is *coughs* is when you wake
in the half-light, and there's part of an old glass, water by the bed,
like someone thought.

As she said, *we don't have much time left, nor must we hurry.*
So, here, have some more of the tea I can't have, you know
it does the pot good to feel warm again.

THE LANGUAGE
All the words and punctuation from Robert Creeley's 'The Language'

Aching again, I want
you To care

in words. for some-
Speech is *love*,

mouth *I love,*
you take so much.

Teeth bite holes
and hurt.

Not Words then,
but eyes, full

of what is
emptiness to fill.

I fill it where
words Locate *you*

and everything
heard, so say a little.

HOW WOULD YOU LIKE (AFTER ALFRED & GUINEVERE)
  — for KMcA
  'how would you like to find
  your bed full of raw oysters?'
    —James Schuyler

how would you like to have to
be as polite as an owl, you screed!?

how would you like to be left hanging
in the back porch with the old coats?

how would you like to be tied
to a snow pole on the Tomintoul road?

how would you like to reprise your MacBeth
on Sugar Mountain, you balloon, you?

how would you like me to cloud
your *lux brumalis* all winter long?

how would you like to look
around the party for the arsehole,
and the arsehole's you!?

how would you like to be
banged up in a dovecot?

how would you like to be
a collie dog herding waves?

how would you like me to give you
a quilt so lovely it made you angry?

how would you like to be the one left
holding the monkey's paw of trauma?

how would you like to wear
a dead incarnation in your buttonhole?

T-H-E-D-O-G
for barney

the dog discovers sea but doesn't understand water

the dog paws his nose against streams of whipped sand

the dog rolls his eyes as I work his ruff

the dog sees me tucked up with a bundle of sighs

the dog has to lick all the salt off his trousers

the dog's sick is froth & water

the dog's got no idea what to do with a bone but bury it

the dog plays hide & seek around the upturned boat-sheds

the dog sticks his snout in and out of the carriage's sliding doors

the dog nose-surfs out the car window

the dog bends his ear in half a scratch

the old bog licks his tail

the dog lays on the toy blue-tit emitting a steady stream of birdsong
  out of his behind

the blind dog worships my SAD lamp

their little puppy is eating his first snow

BUT THAT HAS NOTHING TO DO WITH POETRY

the poem is a means to see one another in our selves
but that has nothing to do with poetry

the poem threads the torn subject
but that has nothing to do with poetry

the poem is a transit bus between idiom and idiolect
but that has nothing to do with poetry

the poem is a route-map through daily complexity
but that has nothing to do with poetry

the poem renders breath as a series of hops and strides
but that has nothing to do with poetry

the poem is performed on stage for sweeties
but that has nothing to do with poetry

the poem is a magic junction in thinking
but that has nothing to do with poetry

the poem is a black sun or tinsel sphincter
but that has nothing to do with poetry

the poem is often repeatable, seldom renewable
but that has nothing to do with poetry

the poem is a dream that doubles seeing
but that has nothing to do with poetry

poems are prose with benefits
but that has nothing to do with poetry

* Some lines inspired by comments made by poets in Anselm Berrigan (ed): *What is Poetry? (Just Kidding, I Know You Know): Interviews from the Poetry Project Newsletter* (Wave Books, 2017)

AFTER FITTERMAN'S 'NOTES ON CONCEPTUALISM'
after Wystan Curnow

pre-text

  I read you

post-text

  I wrote you

hyper-text

  where are you?

paratext

  I'm after you!

AFTER DOTTY LASKY

poets should get back to eating
   crazy shit

poets should get back to cooking
   crazy shit

poets should get back to growing
   crazy shit

poets should lay off hating
   crazy shit

THE LETTER

we have asked you
to attend an
open mediation

before you come
we must insist
that you confirm

how, in every aspect
and every detail,
you are wrong

LET'S AGREE
> *"How did it get to this? Why haven't we spoken in a year? Let's make an agreement."*
>
> — Wes Anderson, *The Darjeeling Limited*

let's agree, not sealions
  but lions by the sea

let's agree on swimming the strokes
  but not counting the laps

let's agree that, in the pilot's eyes,
  night doesn't fall, night rises

let's agree the swing brings your smile
  in and out of focus

let's agree tree-climbing lions
  love to loll on branches

let's agree on intentionality

let's agree on freedom of movement

let's agree to open the window
  let out the damp

let's agree there will be bands of snrain
  some falling as psnow

let's agree, there was a day, *ad infinitum,*
  to live un-alone, to infinity

let's agree on the dozy moss blanket
   of Ballochbuie as a dowry

let's agree gold doesn't shiver
   but vows made by the tide ebb

let's agree, every bird is a specialist

let's agree to know the difference:
   words we can't say /
   words we don't mean

let's agree, you need one pillow for sleeping
   and another pillow for pummelling

let's agree that rage is a blanch

let's agree on applying iodine to *everything*

let's agree on being understanding the first time
   but, when the second blow comes, call a policeman

let's agree that the troll stomps the bed on her fists
   because she wants to learn how to be friends

let's agree those wee head-butts you loved,
   they were lovely because play dissolves fury

let's agree self-hatred is a knife:
   if you sign another pale scar I'll do the same

let's agree that the figure of the father
   can be painted as patrician, or sung as sylvan

let's agree how Dad would have laughed
   if he'd seen the minister was wearing
   a Scotland strip underneath his vestments

let's agree with Gabin: there's a difference between
   being tough and being brave

let's agree that half the story is half true

let's agree gossip is *typical* – not political

let's agree that voice in our head belongs
   to the enemy

let's agree plan A: a dog, a happy life, Fife;
   (let's veto plan B: to flee)

let's agree with Terrance: *"do it right"*

let's agree with Ally, that he wasn't surprised,
   except by the thing that surprised him –
   (and there's more where that came from)

let's agree, the last one standing at the Bauhaus
   house-party was Luca Frei

let's agree to keep a poet on each shoulder:
  "*The Worrier*", "*The Encourager*"

let's agree on two minutes of kindness

let's agree to stay off twitter x

let's agree on the latest amazing colour
  poured from out the moon-cup

let's agree to get over our shelves

let's agree on The List of Doom

let's agree to write a series of comic one-act plays
  for when the bus-drivers swop shifts

let's agree that each member of the band
  plays himself

let's agree that Suffolk isn't the end of the world
  only an orison

let's agree to scatter Brice Marden's ashes
  on Cold Mountain

let's agree to keep a strong centre
  so's to blow around in the wind

let's agree on Labour's new Brexit policy:
   the downward facing dog

let's agree the whole country
   is always England

let's agree that Brexit is the Teignmouth Electron
   of politics

let's agree with the old Communist joke:
   Brexit brought us to the edge of the abyss
   – then we made a bold leap!

let's agree with David Cameron:
   you'd have to be a cross of Einstein, Wittgenstein
   and Mother Theresa to do that job

let's agree with Nick: all politicians will speak
   perfect Gaelic with a Chinese accent

let's agree on the Glaswegian for peloton:
   'awrabikes'

let's agree: eggs on the table

let's agree on broccoli

let's agree that happiness is slimming

let's agree that ginger is a vegetable, but
  it belongs with the apples

let's agree to ask at the Co-op for the ingredients
  to make a chicken

let's agree that junket is a concoction of milk
  and magic

let's agree the sundial has a finger
  up the sun's hole

let's agree with my Indian lover who smiled saying,
  "it's the same all over"

let's agree your last old man crush wasn't me
  but Ludwig, *der Märchenkönig*

let's agree on tucking in the furtive corners
  of the bedsheet very, very, carefully

let's agree that soap can't work when it's dry,
  soup's no good when it's cold

let's agree that someday I will be the kefir king

let's agree that life without cordial seems impossible

let's agree that love is not a judge: to love is to engage

FROM THE SAYINGS OF CHAIRMAN MCGINN
'we have a dream'
— BA Robertson

Don't get ahead – of what?
–*yourself*, of course!

Be the wee guy inside
who's getting excited –

but always keep a lid
on the heid. And then,

only then, you'll come home
to your summer fruits.

TWO PLACE-NAME LOVE-POEMS

THE YELLOW MOUNTAIN
> *'If you are the yellow mountain*
> *I am the red arms of lichen'*
>   — Octavio Paz, translated by Eliot Weinberger

if you are the blue hill
  I am heathen stone

if you are Allt na Gaothain
  I am spindrift

if you are Allt a' Mhòir Ghrianaich
  I am watersmeet

if you are Càrn a' Gheòidh
  I am coming feather-by-feather

if you reach Sunhoney in time
  I will still the summer moon

if you are in Claisnean
  I will lie near you

if you spill by the River Avon
  what will I do then my bright one?

A FOOL'S MIND

I could scatter
  the clouds over
    Am Monadh Ruadh

blow the thistle-
  down off Tom
    Chluaran

shine each last leaf
  on the birches of
    Coire nan Craobh-bheithe

pluck you a flake
  of sharp flint
    from Blàr nan Saighead

plait you the tale
  of a crepuscular tiger
    in Fluich Adagan

wrap the stone
  with new wool
    by Allt nan Cuigeal

warm the White Calf
  in the snows
    of The Brown Cow

gather the rose
  from the fold
    of Allt Fileachaidh

carry you safe
  over the Water
    Splash

find where or whether
  the hazels grow by fleet
    Allt Challa

but mending a fool's
  mind's something
    I cannot do

PLACE-NAME POEMS
for David Wheatley

Maighdean Mhonaidh
the Lassie on the Hill

I placed my finger
  there –

on the flower
  of the mountain

*

Coire Sùileagach
the Eyeful Corrie

see these wee pools, they love
  to lie like this

so the light gets a lift
  off their darkness

*

Allt Phouple
Shelter Burn

safe from
  sucking winds

a form flowers
  by the burn

*

AVAGERILL
  Ballsack Ford

the water rose
  right up to here!

but, please God,
  no further

*

BAD NAN DEARCAG
  Wee-berry Thicket

work your way through
  the berry-patch

til your hands
  and lips turn blue

*

ABERGELDIE
  Brightmouth

the first light greets
  the frozen air

GEALLAIG
Gleamer

the first rays enter
  a burnished water

CAMPING
after Arne Naess

I made myself a tent
with small holes
cut in the fabric

falling asleep
I could still see
the mountains

but the holes
couldn't be shut
so I was freezing

that was the first
of many, many
stupid things

THE CARAVAN BRIDE

Shush your sleepless self. Bend
under the branches, reach out
and touch the wrinkly fingers

of the burn where it's flown
past trust. Shush, listen –
is that a fawn barking

up the hill, or laughter (prime
sound!): whichever it is,
sleep will (<u>won't</u>) be 'us'.

I will shush and stumble
into a firebreak in the night
that anneals fear in the dawn.

I'll be a caravan bride
lit up in flames, as bliss fires
a beautiful fucking comet

in flight. I'll play it back:
(i) polaris is blushing beetroot
 (calamitous), (ii) trauma is un-

hitched in a car shunt (precious),
(iii) the truthiness in the wheel-
chair joke – that we'll take turns pushing

(you knew I would). Shush,
truth's a wish, willing to speak
when the paper's in a knot.

LOCH DUILLEAG-BHÀITE

there are the flags
round the margin
and, for Shōnagon,

some lilies drifting
flower cups among
a fam of flat pads

yes, you *must* swim
around the open water,
but first, get down

through the stems,
stepping in silt
and roiling roots.

HUTOPIANISM
for—and now in memoriam—Gerry Loose

I

CARBETH

Gerry says *it's just*
a wee felt-roofed hut,
a shame to stay inside
but there is rain
wisps of white smoke

rise straightforwardly
from the chimley,
those yaffles
must be trying
to laugh their way in

II

INSHRIACH
for Day

it takes one
of us to
find the hut

and the other
to allow us
to arrive

then we
settle
like snow

III

   for Guy

huts are not what Wittgenstein,
   Heidegger, and Thoreau

had in common
   but what separated them

IV

measure from a man's body
   and you get a hut

measure from his purse
   and you get a house

measure from his army
   and you get a palace

AM BOTHAN AS FHAIDE AIR FALBH– THE FAR HUT
praise poem for the 12-hut Hutopian by Sweeney Bogbum

There it is, her homeless home
at the end of an endless track,

where she goes to be unknown
among safer strangers, to let

her secret selves glimmer and fade
by the fireside. There's new uses

for old news; there's narrow bunks
that dawn on a snicked skyline;

patient boots that snooze,
fearless of creaks and rattles.

But what of the fears that follow
in our footsteps? The fears that

won't take a match, fizzle in mist,
or float off on the elusive tide?

Is there one hut farther on, some
wee Hebride, an unhidden dwelling

with skewy walls and dewy truths,
where terror shall never enter,

where, seeing it all, we're like
Po Chü-i, as he feels his mind settle

BILLIA CROO (GRID-CONNECTED WAVE TEST SITE, ORKNEY)
for Herr Professor Alistair Peebles

(after Barry Cunliffe)

culture is richest where
there's the greatest ratio

  land : *coast*

    o

this patch of the western
ocean's coruscating garden

recalls my favourite song
(mishearing) *the sea's very hum-*

drum ... – but no, there's not
one ocean, not when such an

infinite mix of blues can
outshine the map's cerulean

    o

the sea is there for a solan
to push his wings against

or plunge in, reinventing
the medium – when the light

comes right through them
the waves let's slip wrack

and tangle, pitching round
until they go breaking on

the boulder beach, crashing
under Row Head, hassling

brittlestars and urchins, or splash
near the shelducks dozing

on their green shelf of sun –
there's no need to worry

that any wave is wasted
when there's all this motion

°

along the bay there's
the promise of a new world

from each new device connect-
ed to the cable that runs

out under the wild rocks,
into the diamond space

inside those three buoys –

this is where the metal

gets salt-wet: and that's
the only true test – the problem

is elastic: what kind of roots
will grip fast with moorings

subject to ebb, flood, flux,
in a surge of such force?

     °

what's solid was once liquid
as with rock and sand

which nature divided –
like us – these waves were

tugged and formed, in
slowness, slowness that

we've lost, for there's no
way to relearn the tide's

happy knack of infinitesimal
growth, except by sloshing

around, or waiting, stranded,
on the heave of the moon

A TREE SPEAKS

You know how a tree grows:
   by decisions and divisions –
     some of them 'wrong'.

As shyness is nice
   we stand a bit apart –
     which helps the whole

wood. You've to wait
   months for warmth,
     then split your cones

and whoosh! scatter seed.
   Then you've a choice:
     either cling to the trunk

or climb, branch-over-
   branch, up there,
     where the canopies

pull-out their pockets
   and fill the air
     with birdsong.

TREES ARE Y'S

I can learn from these
  caches of birches   to keep
    a close distance   –some

friendships can last
  a life   –or see
    these various *sorbus*   each

with fingers that are fam-
  iliars of some place
    –or how the mapleish

canopies pipe such
  ambient colours   –for all
    that bare winter's sure

to come   crinkling &
  killing all these leaves   say
    after me: dying's

bound to be toxic
  for some   for some
    death's an adaptation

(Dawyck)

BE THE BEAR (AT MY BEDSIDE)

witness
is a bear
bring it

inside
this dank
patch of duff

fetch
the creeps
a fair cuff

it isn't 'instinct'
for a bear
to cower

give it
leaves to hide
those wild eyes

mustn't be
seen being
my bear's

let me sleep
be me safe
by your bearside

TAIGH NA CAILLICHE

I still recall her rages
and those teeny fists.

But there were hours
lolling in an orchard;

a candle lit at Christmas;
the time she tipped in

Allt Slapin to fish out
a chittering lamb;

and a long walk made
out of kindness over

a moor I couldn't reach.
Muffled in a parka,

fording her wee legs
through the cold river,

in spite of the spate.
While I hid safe in

the distance, something
will cease, something eases.

TWO PATHS (INSHRIACH)

I

we have been
to the end
of the path

and are ready
for our beds
and dreams

of pillow hills
a firm staff
in our hands

and the inclin-
ation to leave
old arguments

II

on our last morning
she led me down

the path
through the wood

that led
to The Mountain

where it had lain
in wait all week long

AFTER GEDDES
for Day

what's that
  in the darkness?

  what's that
through the window?

what's that
  coming closer?

what's that
  in flight?

LIONS

Let's go to the sea then
   where you're safe to love me.

Let's be lions with lionhearts,
   lionpride, lioneyes.

Let's be the kind of lion
   who knows all sorts, like
   how the sea just flows.

Let's flick through the property pages,
   find a den by the strand
   and settle down.

Let's have a tree-swing
   at the end of the garden.

Let's be wary, for lions are kind
   one-to-one but cruel in the circus.

Let's free you, Lion, of your fears
   of *them*, all the painted clowns.

But let's never happens
   for fright this deep always wins.

HERE'S AN EMPTINESS WE COULD SHARE
— on a Korean vase

Her words hide like clouds.
   His glaze shines like the sky.

Weathers change: whether
   we're light or murky.

I'll remain empty enough
   to let you in

if you remain open enough
   to pour out everything.

AVOCADO (I)

she peels and pins
  the stones

  sets them on the sill
like a cluster

of tiny rockets
  each one fuelled

  by its own
glass of water

AVOCADO (II)

I still give each stone
  a chance of life

so as to remember
  how innocence

can float over it's
  own wetness

or be pinned in the whim
   of an atmosphere

NOCTURNE

The tear in the old sheets
shows I've been sleeping

in the middle of the bed
for far too long. This

new blue linen, it's
darker than blue eyes,

dark as the night skies.
To the touch the stars

have left a hundred
thousand scratches

which, so I'm told, should
come out in the wash.

RIFFING ON ENSLIN

Isn't that what we all want?
to live in a friend's room

with their books and their plants,
a towel on the rippled shores

of the radiator, not knowing
their worries, just resting
  in their light

MAKE MEND

maybe she says
we're not broken

maybe she says
we're fragile

maybe she says
we're kintsugi

maybe she says
in the making

SADFACE
 for GF

The doctor writer's brung
a doctor's question:

*what are you looking
forward to this winter?*

But it doesn't really work
like that– not with pain days,

what with rain days, bugs,
(no meds), walks

hemmed in. For Hope
not to become a lash, what

I'm looking forward to
this winter, doc, is Love.

TWO BAYS

KINGHORN
> *what love could learn from such a sight*
> *'Who cares for daisies.*
> *Do you hear me.*
> *Yes I can hear you.*
> *Very well then explain.*
> *That I care for daises.*
> *That we care for daisies.*
> *Come in come in.*
> *Yes and I will not cry.'*
> — Gertrude Stein, *Every Afternoon, a Dialogue*

that first day
  on the sunshone beach
    let's get wed set

us careening in
  rings by the Skellies
    laughing *yes*

yes yes   we leaned
  our heads back
    pillowed on a mud-

stone rock beneath
  Carlinhead and marked
    an old couple

doddle down how each
  of his s l o w
    swim-strokes

were watched by her
  patient red towel
    tucked waiting

under a crooked
  arm   as we watched
  ourselves watch

her watching him
  reading the day's
    lesson in the labour

of waiting   for
  the waiting supposed
    to come   I couldn't

want for anything
  more than waiting
    for our part

of their shared time
  which this past
    year's undone

Rackwick

she wants us
　to live here　where
　　she begins to leave

in the tumult
　as Rackwick's
　　boulder beach is

sporadically sorted
　by what the cliffs
　　disdain

the stack stands
　being broken
　　in time　I see

her over again
　hooded against
　　the water*sky*　be-

coming alone
　fought over
　　again　forced

again to flee
　by the upwell-
　　ing sea　as a last

thrown stone
  to skim *is*
    there? is gone

CODA

it would have been
  a kinder ending if you'd
    crept in The Dwarfie Stane

leaving me in the protection
  of the sea eagle
    and her warden

THE BIRCH
> *'Loving you so*
> *I was too blind to see you*
> *Letting me go...'*
> — Laura Nyro, *It's Gonna Take a Miracle*

this is love's last
task: to shimmy
the sharp railings

clamber down to
the birch where
we met and trowel

out a hole for our
blue-flowered teapot
which holds my ring

and a card post-
marked in Dutch:
love we will always

catch each other
you'll be pleased
to know two years

on our tree is
fulfilling its purpose –
disseminating light

and protection,
accepting leaves
only grow

and fall because
they can't know
how it ends

THE CATCH

when we met I showed her
how to play with a ball

and a wall and laughing
throw with the anger

buried inside her
until the ball went flying

over my head and soon
after our playing ended

POOR.OLD.

a kiss isn't
a kiss un-

less it meets
its reflection

        art is perfect but
        without the im-

        perfections of a self
        who's seeing?

didn't walking
into the arms

of the digger
tell you something?

        the pips & core
        you gave the pony

        were yours for
        the eating

LYRIC

I am a frame
of bone
the winds

would sound
in but for
the blood

that whines
through the bed
of my heart

GRAVE POEMS

14.III.2011

how much more
  than halfway?

rolled buds
  on my birthday

14.III.20

time
  adds
    a stone

to
  blossom
    & pollen

14.III.21

the lesson
  of life is

what heals us
  is kindness

14.III.24

to have
a share in
  spring

meaning so
much in so
little
  again

M
ORN
ING
EVE
NIN
G

ACKNOWLEDGEMENTS

Thanks to the editors and publishers of the little magazines, journals, catalogues, blogs, art projects, exhibitions, and websites in which these poems first appeared. 'After Dante, The Inferno, Canto 13', composed for a memorial to Michael Stanley, Campbell Park, Milton Keynes, commissioned by MK Gallery (2019). 'let me remind you (the dream poem)': from *Poetry* magazine. Earlier versions of the poems on Stonypath, including 'Sea Eck', 'Lochan Eck', 'new model glider', 'family', 'inheritance', and 'broken dishes', from *Question Your Teaspoons* (Calder Wood Press, 2012), and *New Arcadians Journal* No. 61/62, 2007. 'A child's drawings for verse' refers to the booklet, *The Axis*, with poems by Ian Hamilton Finlay, and drawings by 9-year-old Eck Finlay (Wild Hawthorn Press, 1975). 'A Charm Against Domestic Violence', from the anthology, *Masculinity, an anthology of Modern Voices*, (Broken Sleep, 2023). 'The yellow mountain': from *Some Colour Trends* (Deveron Projects, 2014). 'a fool's mind', 'place-name poems', from *gathering: a place-aware guide to the Cairngorms*, (Hauser & Wirth, 2018). 'Camping', from the artist blog, *còmhlan bheanntan, a company of mountains*, commissioned by Atlas Arts, Isle of Skye, 2013. Some of the Hutopian poems are from *Hutopia*, a book accompanying "Machines à Penser, Prada Fondazione, 2018 Architecture Biennale. 'Billia Croo' and 'homage to Velimir Khlebnikov', from *ebban an' flowan* (with Alistair Peebles and Laura Watts, 2015). An earlier version of Avocado (I) appeared in *New Writing Scotland*, No. 37. 'The Birch', from Petrichor magazine. A few entries in 'Let's agree' were composed in collaboration with Daisy Lafarge. 'morningevening', from *aswirl* magazine, No. 1. Some of the shorter poems appeared on *dailies*, a daily poem, https://dailies.substack.com.

Notes for two place-name love poems. THE YELLOW MOUNTAIN: this poem wanders The Cabrach and Cairngorms, with deviations around West Aberdeenshire. Heathen stone: dark mark in granite; Allt na Gaothain, *Snow-drift Burn*; Allt a' Mhòir Ghrianaich, *Sunnyside Burn*; Càrn a' Gheòidh, *Goose Cairn*; William Alexander speculates Sunhoney is Sidhean a' Chonnaidh, *Seats of the Firewood,* stone circle framing the standstill moon every 18.6 years. Claisnean, *Lassie's Cleft*; River Avon, *Brightwater*, where Ath-fhinn drowned. Sources include: William Alexander: *The Place-Names of Aberdeenshire*; Peter Drummond: email to AF; Edward Dwelly: *The Illustrated Gaelic-English Dictionary*; James Macdonald: *The Place Names of West Aberdeenshire*; Adam Watson and Elizabeth Allan: *The Place Names of Upper Deeside.* A FOOL'S MIND also wanders the Cairngorms. It is inspired by Andrew Schelling's translation of a poem by the 14th century Kashmiri poet Lal Ded. Tom Chluaran, *Thistle Knowe*, on Sròn Dubh. Coire nan Craobh-bheithe, *Birch Trees Corrie*, west of Lochnagar. Blàr nan Saighead, *The Arrows Moss*, Glen Feshie. Fliuch-adagan, *The Wetted Rush-stooks*, Glen Feshie. Allt nan Cuigeal, *Distaffs Burn*, refers to spindles for winding wool, rises on the Shank of Corn Arn, Glen Tanar. The White Calf, snow wreath in the corrie of Brown Cow Hill. Allt Fileachaidh, *Pleat Burn*, or *Burn of the Fold*, possibly referring to a bent corrie below Creag na Slabhraidh, Glen Muick. The Water Splash, crossing Allt a' Mhadaidh, Glen Lui. Allt Challa, *Hazel Burn?* Adam Watson notes other possible interpretations, *defeat, hard-water,* or *meadow.* Sources: William Alexander: *The Place-Names of Aberdeenshire*; Peter Drummond: email to AF; Edward Dwelly: *The Illustrated Gaelic-English Dictionary*, James Macdonald: *The Place Names of West Aberdeenshire;* Richard Perry: *In the High Grampians*; Andrew Schelling: *Love and The Turning Seasons*; Adam Watson and Elizabeth Allan: *The Place Names of Upper Deeside.* Thanks to Ron Brander, and Gill Russell.

LAY OUT YOUR UNREST

www.ingramcontent.com/pod-product-compliance
Lightning Source LLC
Chambersburg PA
CBHW020857160426
43192CB00007B/956